TEEN Pioneers

YOUNG PEOPLE WHO HAVE CHANGED THE WORLD

Ben Hubbard

W

FRANKLIN WATTS

LONDON • SYDNEY

Franklin Watts
First published in Great Britain in 2019 by
The Watts Publishing Group
Copyright © The Watts Publishing
Group 2019

Credits
Editor: Julia Bird
Designer: Mo Choy

ISBN 978 1 4451 6368 0

Picture credits:
Ted Aljibe/AFP/Getty Images: 45. Sarah Armas/Shutterstock: 19. Aurora Photos/
Alamy: 54. Behrouz Badrouj/©Women Make Movies/Courtesy Everett Collection/
Alamy: 7. Maxim Blinkov/Shutterstock: 53. Bye Bye Plastic Bags: 52, 55. Debrajoti
Chakraborty/NurPhoto/Getty Images: 43. Flora Charner courtesy of narrative.ly:
12. Coloursinmylife/Shutterstock: 29, 31. Istvan Csak/Shutterstock: 46. Michael
Desmond/ABC via Getty Images: 10. DPA/Alamy: 48. Jerome Favre/EPA-EFE/
REX/Shutterstock: 28, 30. Foto24/Gallo Images/Getty Images: 38. Rokhsareh
Ghaemmaghami/©Women Make Movies/Courtesy Everett Collection/Alamy: 6.
Aude Guerrucci-Pool/Getty Images: 56. Wael Hamzeh/EPA/REX/Shutterstock:
25. Courtesy the Hu family: 60. John Lamparski/WireImages/GettyImages: 32.
Justin Lane/EPA/REX/Shutterstock: 24. Michael Loccisano/Getty Images for
Nickelodeon: 26. Saul Loeb/AFP/Getty Images: 11. Frances R. Malasig/EPA/REX/
Shutterstock: 44. Robin Marchant/Getty Images: 16. Kevin Mazur/Getty Images
for CNN: 20. David Paul Morris/Bloomberg via Getty Images: 50. Robert Onecini/
Shutterstock: 33. Ehab Othman/Shutterstock: 47. Pacific Press/Light Rocket
via Getty Images: 41. Aamir Qureshi/AFP/Getty Images: 23. Luiz Rampelotto/
EuropaNewswire/Alamy: 9. Jonne Roriz/Sports Illustrated/Getty Images: 15.
Debra L Rothenberg/Getty Images: 40. Antonio Scorza/AFP/Getty Images: 14.
Enid M. Salgado: 18. Antony Stanley/WENN/Alamy: 58. Jordan Strauss/Invision/
AP/REX/Shutterstock: 36. Michael Stewart/Getty Images: 37. Justin Tallis/AFP/
Getty Images: 49. Veronique de Vigurie/Getty Images: 22. WENN/Alamy: 34.

Every attempt has been made to clear copyright. Should there be any
inadvertent omission please apply to the publisher for rectification.

Franklin Watts
An imprint of
Hachette Children's Group
Part of The Watts Publishing Group
Carmelite House
50 Victoria Embankment
London EC4Y 0DZ

An Hachette UK Company
www.hachette.co.uk
www.franklinwatts.co.uk

FSC
www.fsc.org
MIX
Paper from
responsible sources
FSC® C104740

Contents

What does it mean to be a pioneer?

In the past, pioneers were the first people to travel and settle in distant lands. In more recent times, pioneers are those who create or develop something – a new piece of technology, an organisation, a different way of thinking about things. A pioneer, then, can be described as the first person to do something new.

The 21 pioneers in this book have been picked not only because they were the first to do something new, but also because of their age when they did it. Each one made a great pioneering change to the world and they did so as a teenager. Their young age is what makes the accomplishments of these pioneers all the more impressive.

Age is not the only thing that unites the teen pioneers in the following pages. They also all wanted to help others. Some did this by developing drugs to detect disease, building Braille printers for the blind or creating affordable robotic arms for amputee victims. Others set up organisations to send recycled glasses to undeveloped countries, pay for the education of girls in poverty or provide hurricane victims with solar lamps to see at night. Several teen pioneers became activists who spoke out against forced marriages, human trafficking and the discrimination of lesbian, gay, bisexual and transgender people.

However they did it, each pioneer found a way to make things better and break new ground. In this way, the teenagers in this book are the new pioneers of our modern age.

THESE INSPIRATIONAL STORIES SHOW YOU CAN ACHIEVE AMAZING THINGS AT ANY AGE.

BE INSPIRED!

Sonita Alizadeh

"The older generations,
they are teaching us
these old traditions.
But we can change them.
Not all of them. But some."

NAME: Sonita Alizadeh
BORN: 1997
PLACE OF BIRTH: Herat,
Afghanistan
ROLE: Rapper and Activist
Against Forced Child Marriage

The Child Bride

Sonita Alizadeh was ten years old when her parents said she would be a bride. An older man had offered to pay to marry Sonita and her family needed the money. But at the last minute, the marriage was called off. Instead, Sonita's family fled the war in their native Afghanistan for neighbouring Iran. But on the way, they were stopped by soldiers who threatened to kidnap Sonita if they were not given money. After paying, Sonita's family finally reached Iran and safety.

Afghan Refugee

In Tehran, the capital of Iran, Sonita was given a place at a school for Afghan refugees. Sonita cleaned the school toilets to earn money. At the school, Sonita met other Afghan girls who would soon be forced to marry. Over 15 per cent of Afghan females are forced to marry before they turn 15, although this is illegal. The friends would discuss the price they would be sold for: some US$3,000, others US$12,000. Once married, the girls would be expected to cook, clean and bear children. Some Afghan child brides suffer violence and abuse from their husbands.

Rap Inspiration

One day when she was cleaning, Sonita heard some music that would change her life: rap. Soon she was writing her own raps about the injustice of child brides being sold to the highest bidder. Sonita dreamed of recording her rap music and becoming a star, like Eminem or Iranian rapper, Yas. But in Iran, it is illegal for women to be singers. No one dared risk recording Sonita. Worse news was to follow. Sonita's mother had found her a husband in Afghanistan. He would pay US$9,000 to marry the now 16-year-old Sonita.

MARRIAGE MONEY

Sonita's mother demanded that she return to Afghanistan to marry. The money being offered was needed for Sonita's brother to buy his own bride. If Sonita returned to marry she would have to abandon her life, education and dreams of being a rapper. But luck was on her side. A filmmaker making a documentary about Sonita offered to pay US$2,000 if her mother postponed Sonita's marriage. Her mother agreed.

BRIDES FOR SALE

Things began to change for Sonita. A producer agreed to record her rap song 'Brides for Sale'. The song challenges Afghan women to stand up to the system of forced child marriages. Sonita made a video for the song and posted it on YouTube. In two days it received thousands of views. Sonita then entered her song into a US competition. To her amazement, she won. The prize was US$1,000, which Sonita gave to her mother.

> "I am 15 years old, from Herat.
> A few have come as suitors and I am confused/I am perplexed by this tradition and these people.
> They sell girls for money.
> No right to choose."
>
> – 'Brides for Sale', Sonita Alizadeh

AMERICAN OFFER

Soon there was even better news. The video was seen by an American organisation which offered Sonita a scholarship to study at a high school in Utah, USA. But first, Sonita would have to apply for a passport in Afghanistan. If she returned to her home country, Sonita feared she would never leave. But she had no choice. After travelling to Afghanistan, Sonita visited her family. Her mother and brothers were embarrassed by her song, but her nieces and nephews already knew it by heart.

8

Rapping Activist

Sonita's passport finally arrived after months of waiting in the war-torn Afghan capital of Kabul. But it was only when she reached Utah that Sonita plucked up the courage to tell her mother about the scholarship. Despite this, Sonita thrived in the USA. She learned English, made many friends and performed her rap to sold-out audiences. Her 'Brides for Sale' video has been watched over a million times and today Sonita is a famous activist raising awareness about forced child marriage. She speaks at conferences around the USA and is often interviewed by the international media. Sonita hopes her pioneering work in speaking out about forced marriages will help change attitudes around the world.

Forced Marriage

- Between 60% and 80% of married Afghan women are in forced marriages
- In developing countries, 1 in 9 girls are married before the age of 15
- Over 650 million women in the world today were married as children

United Nations Population Fund

Mikaila Ulmer

Bee Terrified

When Mikaila Ulmer was four years old, she was terrified of bees. Then she was stung twice in one week! Mikaila's parents suggested she should learn about bees instead of being scared of them. She discovered that bees are an essential part of our ecosystem, and pollinate many of the plants on Earth. Mikaila was shocked to learn that bees are in danger of extinction. She decided to try to help save the bees.

NAME: Mikaila Ulmer
BORN: 2004
PLACE OF BIRTH:
Austin, Texas, USA
ROLE: Entrepreneur,
Educator, Bee ambassador

Honey Sweetener

Around the time Mikaila was stung, she received a cookbook from her great grandmother. The cookbook contained a recipe for lemonade with honey. This gave Mikaila an idea. She made jugs of lemonade sweetened with honey and set up a lemonade stand at a fair in her hometown of Austin, Texas. She sold out. At the next year's fair, she sold out again. Everyone wanted Mikaila's lemonade!

Mikaila's work brought her into contact with then US President Barack Obama.

"If the bee disappeared off the face of the globe then man would only have four years of life left."
– Albert Einstein, scientist

MIKAILA AND THE BEES

- Me & the Bees Lemonade is sold at over 300 shops across the USA

- Mikaila also runs a bee charity called the Healthy Hive Foundation

- Mikaila's parents and brothers all work for her

- Mikaila is writing a book for children about starting your own business.

Business of Bees

Before Mikaila knew it, her lemonade was big business. In 2014, she appeared on the US TV show 'Shark Tank' (far left), where business people invest in entrepreneurs' ideas. Mikaila secured a US$60,000 investment and a contract with American supermarket, Whole Foods. Her lemonade was soon sold across the USA. But for Mikaila, it is not just about making money. For every bottle of lemonade sold, 10 per cent goes to organisations that help bees.

Rene Silva

NAME: Rene Silva
BORN: 1993
PLACE OF BIRTH: Rio de Janeiro, Brazil
ROLE: Journalist, Newspaper editor, Community activist

Editor's Access

In 2016, journalist Rene Silva was reporting on the forced eviction of residents from the slum neighbourhoods of Complexo do Alemão in Rio de Janeiro, Brazil. But the police did not want the media present and things became violent. As Rene used his mobile phone to live-broadcast the events, he was pepper-sprayed, handcuffed and arrested. The police then fired tear gas and rubber bullets to warn others away. For Rene Silva, editor of newspaper *Voz da Comunicades* (*Community Voice*), the incident was nothing new.

"It [the newspaper] says what the residents want to say and what they aren't able to say through the large media outlets, because I don't believe the large media has a channel that's really linked into the community."

Printing the News

Rene Silva was only 11 when he created *Voz da Comunicades*. His aim was to report on the issues facing the 200,000 residents of Complexo do Alemão, a Rio hillside area containing 19 slums known as favelas. In the evening, Rene wrote articles at the dinner table in his small home in Alemão (far left). The single-page newspaper was then printed out at Rene's school, and given out around the neighbourhood. By the time Rene was 14, *Voz da Comunicades* had a readership of 5,000 people.

Gang Owned

For many decades before the launch of *Voz da Comunicades,* Complexo do Alemão was well-known to be one of Rio's most dangerous areas. Made up of crammed-together brick homes, Alemão was controlled by two of the city's most powerful gangs who trafficked drugs and ruled over local residents like kings. Instead of paying taxes, the people of Alemão had to pay the gang lords fees to receive basic services such as electricity and water.

Guns and Tanks

In 2010, the Brazilian government decided to clean up Alemão. Brazil had recently won the bid to host the 2014 FIFA Football World Cup, and was concerned about security in Rio. On 28 November, thousands of armed police raided the favelas. Rene Silva awoke to hear helicopters flying overhead (below), while gun battles broke out between the police and the gangs. Hundreds of journalists covering the raid were ordered out of the area. Rene Silva, however, was in the middle of the action.

Favela Footage

The raid on Alemão was making news around the world. The television footage, however, came only from helicopters or reports from outside the favelas. But Rene and his journalists could provide live reports from inside Alemão via *Voz da Comunicades*' Twitter account. As the raid went on, *Voz*'s Twitter followers exploded from 180 to 29,000. Global media outlets began using the newspaper as their main source of information about the raid. After 72 hours, the raid was over and four people had been killed. Because of Rene, every detail of the raid had been made public worldwide. The community newspaper editor was now internationally famous.

In 2015, Rio de Janeiro was one of South America's most dangerous cities with a murder rate of 38 per 100,000 residents. Most of these murders took place in the favelas.

"When I was younger, I never imagined how big this whole thing could become [...] My young age made things difficult for me. Many people didn't believe I was really the one putting the newspaper together."

COMUNICADES CELEBRITY

Today, Rene Silva is a celebrity both in Alemão and Brazil. He has appeared on numerous television shows and has spoken at many conferences about his experiences. Rene was even chosen as one of the Brazilians to carry the torch at the 2016 Olympic Games in Rio (above). Today, *Voz da Comunicades* has a print run of over 10,000 copies and a staff of 30 people. Despite his fame, reporting on Alemão's community issues remains Rene's main aim: "What led me to become a journalist was the desire to help my community and fight for better living conditions for all who live around here," he said.

Mary Grace Henry

"The greatest obstacle to education faced by both girls and boys is poverty. Girls, though, face a second hurdle that is far more difficult to address: their culture. In many countries throughout the world, girls are viewed as having not just lesser value than boys, but often devastatingly little or no value."

NAME: Mary Grace Henry
BORN: 1997
PLACE OF BIRTH: Harrison, New York, USA
ROLE: Education Campaigner and Business owner

Business of Educating

When Mary Grace Henry was 12 years old she asked for a sewing machine for her birthday. She was going to start her own business sewing and selling headbands. But this was going to be a business with a twist. All of the profits would go to paying for girls in Africa to go to school. In some poorer countries, many families cannot afford to educate all their children. Often, they choose to educate only their sons. Mary decided she would start by paying for the education of one girl in Uganda.

GIRLS AND EDUCATION

- Over 130 million girls in the world between the age of 6 and 17 are out of school
- Over 15 million girls of primary-school age – half of them in sub-Saharan Africa – will never enter a classroom
- Women make up more than two-thirds of the world's 796 million illiterate people.

Reverse the Course

After locking herself away with her sewing machine, Mary made some headbands which were sold through her school bookshop. In two days, her headbands had sold out. Before long, Mary had made enough money to pay for the education of 100 girls in Uganda. Her headbands began selling at local fairs and markets. She named her business 'Reverse the Course' and extended her range of headwear to bows, buttons and ponytail ties. Mary even had to hire people to help with the sewing.

Awards and Africa

Today, Mary has sold over 11,000 headwear items through her website and has products in shops in seven different US states. She has raised tens of thousands of dollars for her cause and helps educate girls in Haiti and Paraguay, as well as Africa. In 2014, Mary won a World of Children Award and visited the girls in Africa that she is helping educate. Mary was thrilled to see the girls were as excited about education as she is.

Salvador Gómez Colón

"One day should not go by that we don't remind ourselves of how we can make other people's lives better."

NAME: Salvador Gómez Colón
BORN: 2002
PLACE OF BIRTH: San Juan, Puerto Rico
ROLE: Fundraiser and social campaigner

The Hurricane Hits

In September 2017, a category-four hurricane struck the Caribbean island of Puerto Rico. Called Maria, the hurricane whipped the island with 250 km/h winds, drenched it with heavy rainfall and caused widespread flash-flooding. In the capital city, San Juan, whole neighbourhoods were destroyed. Fifteen-year-old Salvador Gómez Colón and his family were among the lucky ones: their San Juan apartment had been left standing. Their building had a generator for electricity and a water cistern, but thousands of Puerto Ricans were left without these basic necessities.

Hurricane Maria brought down power lines across Puerto Rico.

CROWDFUNDING

With government officials saying it could take up to a year for power to be restored, Salvador looked for a way to help. He spoke to two family friends: a project worker tackling energy poverty in Africa and a military veteran who had served in Afghanistan. They suggested solar power lamps and hand-crank washing machines could help Puerto Ricans. So Salvador set up an online crowdfunding campaign. Within 24 hours, he had raised US$14,000.

LIGHT AND CLEAN CLOTHES

With the money, Salvador began buying solar lamps and hand-crank washing machines. He enlisted volunteers and family members to help distribute them. To date, Salvador has raised over US$125,000 and donated hundreds of washing machines and over 840 solar lamps to those in need. In recognition of Salvador's work he was named one of *TIME* magazine's most influential teens of 2017. However, the real reward, Salvador says, is from helping others.

Campbell Remess

"The magic in the bears is the hope. It's the hope that the bears give people. It's the best medicine for them."

NAME: Campbell Remess, nickname 'Bumble'
BORN: 2004
PLACE OF BIRTH: Hobart, Australia
ROLE: Bear maker and charity owner

A Pattern for Presents

When Campbell Remess was nine years old, he wanted to take Christmas presents to every sick child at his local hospital in Hobart, Australia. After his parents told him that it would be too expensive, Campbell decided that if he couldn't afford to buy the gifts, he would simply make them. Campbell had never used a sewing machine before, but soon found a pattern online he wanted to use: "I decided to make a teddy bear, because everybody loves teddy bears," Campbell said. Five hours later, Campbell had created his first teddy bear.

Project 365

Campbell's goal was to make one teddy bear every day for a sick child in need, 365 days of the year. His goal would therefore become known as Project 365. Today, Campbell can make one bright, fuzzy teddy bear in just one hour and has made over 1,400 to date. Campbell sends his finished bears to hospitals around the world and also hand delivers them. Seeing children react happily to his bears is important to Campbell.

Cancer Cruises

A few years ago, Campbell had some bad news. His father's recurring cancer had returned. To support his father, Campbell made a special 'winner' bear. Today, Campbell's father is cancer-free. This experience made Campbell reach out to other people suffering from cancer. To help them, Campbell set up Kindness Cruises, a charity which raises money to send cancer sufferers on holiday aboard cruise ships. This made Campbell the youngest owner of a charity in Australia.

School and Celebrity

Campbell's work has made him famous around the world. Campbell's bears won him a CNN Young Wonder award and a video clip of his work became a viral sensation. Today, Campbell's video has been watched over 30 million times and he has requests for bears and interviews from all over the world. So Campbell can still behave like any other teenage boy, his mother has limited the number of interviews he does to one every two days. To cope with the emails and requests on social media, Campbell has his own strategy: "I've got to put it to the side, make the bear, and then I go back on for five minutes and write back to them."

Malala Yousafzai

A LIFE INTERRUPTED

Malala grew up in Pakistan's idyllic Swat Valley, a holiday destination often called the 'Switzerland of Asia'. Here, Malala went to the local school run by her father, and dreamed of becoming a doctor. But in 2007, Taliban militants invaded Swat Valley and everything changed.

NAME: Malala Yousafzai
BORN: 1997
PLACE OF BIRTH: Swat Valley, Khyber Pakhtunkhwa, Pakistan
ROLE: Activist for female education

"I am not against anyone, neither am I here to speak in terms of personal revenge against the Taliban or any other terrorist group. I'm here to speak up for the right of education for every child. I want education for the sons and daughters of the Taliban and all terrorists and extremists."

SEIZING CONTROL

The Taliban is a military group that uses violence to impose a strict form of Islamic law. When the Taliban seized control of Swat Valley they banned television, music and the education of girls. They also blew up 100 schools. Malala, however, refused to be intimidated. She gave a speech at a local press club and demanded: "How dare the Taliban take away my basic rights to education?" Her speech received worldwide media attention. But soon fighting between the Pakistani army and the Taliban made Malala's village too dangerous and her family, and many others, had to flee (above).

TALIBAN TARGET

In 2011, the army forced the Taliban to retreat from Swat Valley and Malala's school reopened. For her work in fighting for girls' education, Malala was made the subject of a New York Times documentary. But her fame made her a target for the Taliban. In October 2012, Malala and her classmates were returning from an exam when a masked gunman boarded their bus. He shouted "Who is Malala?" and then shot her in the head. Malala was rushed to hospital in Peshawar, but her chances of survival were considered slim.

ENGLISH HOSPITAL

After five hours of surgery, doctors were able to remove the bullet which had miraculously missed Malala's brain and lodged in her shoulder. But part of Malala's skull had to be removed and the nerves were severed along one side of her face. By chance, two British doctors were attending a seminar in Peshawar and rushed to help. They recommended Malala be flown to Birmingham, England for post-operative care.

SURGERY AND SPEECHES

It took over three months for Malala to recover. She needed several operations and an implant to restore her hearing. Meanwhile, the shooting of Malala was condemned by world leaders and caused protests in several Pakistani cities. Over two million people signed a petition which led to the first Right to Education Bill in Pakistan. Nine months after the shooting, Malala made a speech calling for worldwide access to education to a packed room at the United Nations, USA on her 16th birthday (right).

"One child, one teacher, one book, one pen can change the world."

NOBEL PEACE PRIZE

Today, Malala is world famous and uses her high profile to campaign for the right to education. For this, she has won countless awards, met with world leaders and written books about her experiences. Then, in 2014, Malala became the youngest ever person to be awarded the Nobel Peace Prize. Malala lives and studies in England and in 2018 visited Pakistan for the first time since the shooting. While there she was asked about the Taliban militants who tried to silence her: "I think they may be regretting that they shot Malala. Now she is heard in every corner of the world," she said.

EDUCATION IN PAKISTAN

• Between 2007 and 2015, there were 867 attacks by Islamist terrorists on Pakistan schools

• Only 3 per cent of Pakistani children who start primary school complete their final year

• Girls from poor families are the least likely children to attend school in Pakistan

• In 2018, the Pakistan government stated it would increase education spending by US$5 billion and target out-of-school children, the poorest and girls.

Yash Gupta

"Vision is an essential part of learning and without it, students are unfairly prevented from achieving their full potential."

NAME: Yash Gupta
BORN: 1996
PLACE OF BIRTH: India
(EMIGRATED TO CALIFORNIA, USA AT 1 YEAR OLD)
ROLE: OWNER OF A NON-PROFIT GLASSES RECYCLING ORGANISATION

Taekwondo Teenager

When Yash Gupta was a young teenager he broke his glasses at taekwondo practice. For the seven days before Yash's new glasses arrived, everything was a blur. Then he learned there were more than 13 million children in the world who don't have the glasses they need.

Random Glasses

Yash's family all wear glasses and he found lots of discarded pairs lying around the house. Yash realised those glasses could help children overseas. With his father's help, Yash set up an organisation called Sight Learning that recycles used glasses. They installed boxes at local optometrists where patients could drop off their old glasses after getting a new pair.

PEOPLE NEED GLASSES

Around 700 million people worldwide need glasses and cannot afford them. Of these 700 million, 13 million are school children. Not having glasses puts these children in a disadvantaged position to learn.

Helping the World to See

Today, Sight Learning has collected and distributed thousands of pairs of glasses overseas. Yash spends 20 hours a week after school collecting and shipping glasses. He has travelled to India and Mexico to deliver the glasses and says this is the best part of the job. For his work, Yash has been honoured with a visit to the White House. However, Yash says he is not the only young person trying to make the world a better place. "I think there's a misconception with our generation. Many of my friends are doing things to improve their communities. Kids are passionate and can make a difference," he said.

Joshua Wong

NAME: Joshua Wong
BORN: 1996
PLACE OF BIRTH:
Hong Kong, China
ROLE: Student activist
and Politician

Street Protests

In 2014, Joshua Wong spent his 18th birthday with thousands of people on the streets of Hong Kong, protesting for their democratic rights. The protestors called themselves the Umbrella Movement and spent three months occupying the city's financial district. But the protests would later have consequences for Joshua.

Hong Kong Handover

Joshua Wong began fighting for human rights after his father took him to visit Hong Kong's homeless people as a child. When he was 15, Joshua formed the group Scholarism to fight for democracy. Hong Kong is a former British colony that was returned to China in 1997. It was promised that the city could continue with a form of self-rule and elect its own officials. But in 2014, the Chinese government imposed limits to Hong Kong's electoral system. Joshua and the Umbrella Movement soon hit the streets in protest.

HONG KONG

After Britain returned Hong Kong to China, the Chinese government agreed to rule the country under 'one country, two systems'. This would give Hong Kong the right to free, democratic elections and its own independent courts. But activists like Joshua say China is imposing its own undemocratic rule under its Communist political system.

Umbrella Movement

The Umbrella Movement got its name because the protestors used umbrellas as shields against the tear gas and pepper-spray being used against them by police. For 79 days the protestors organised peaceful sit-ins across Hong Kong's financial district, which blocked many major roads. The police tried to break up the demonstrations using batons and tear gas. But violence against the protestors simply resulted in many others joining the demonstrations. Protestor numbers reached 100,000 people at one point.

Demosisto Candidate

The Umbrella Movement's protest was watched by people from all over the world, but it did not lead to any political changes. Joshua's next step was to launch his own political party called Demosisto. In 2016, Demosisto's candidate Nathan Law won a seat in Hong Kong's Legislative Council. But in 2017, the Chinese government removed Nathan, saying he had insulted China while he was swearing his oath for office. Soon afterwards, Nathan and Joshua were arrested and jailed for their part in organising the 2014 Umbrella protests.

AWARDS

One of *TIME* magazine's most influential teens of 2014

• One of *Fortune* magazine's greatest leaders, 2015

• Nomination for Nobel Peace Prize, 2018.

Protestors show their support for Joshua and Nathan during their trial.

Prisoners

In prison, Joshua was allowed to subscribe to one newspaper, watch television at mealtimes, and receive letters. The 777 pages of letters he received helped Joshua feel less alone. In 2018, Nathan and Joshua were released from prison, but their sentences mean they cannot stand for public office for five years. For Joshua, being punished is nothing new. Since becoming an activist he has been pelted with eggs, physically assaulted, arrested several times and denied entry to Malaysia and Thailand.

ACCLAIM AND ATTENTION

Today, Joshua fights on for democratic rights in Hong Kong. His work has brought him international acclaim and his articles appear in many prestigious newspapers. A globally-recognised figure, Joshua's fight remains the same: to hold free elections in Hong Kong and for the people to be able to elect their own Legislative Council. Joshua hopes that by having the eyes of the world on Hong Kong, international pressure may make this possible: "Hong Kong can't yet be described as a prison, but it's still an imprisoned place. Why do I see hope? Everybody's on our side," Joshua said.

"They can lock up our bodies, but they can't lock up our minds."

Kelvin Doe

"Creativity is universal and can be found in places where one does not expect to find it. Perseverance and passion are essential to nurturing that creative ability."

NAME: KELVIN DOE
BORN: 1996
PLACE OF BIRTH:
FREETOWN, SIERRA LEONE
ROLE: INVENTOR, ENGINEER
AND DJ

LOOKING FOR LIGHT

When Kelvin Doe was growing up, there was often no electricity in his poor neighbourhood in Freetown, Sierra Leone. "The lights would come on once in a week and the rest of the month dark," Kelvin said. The ten-year-old Kelvin started rummaging in rubbish bins, looking for discarded electronics. After his family had gone to bed Kelvin would stay up late, pulling the electronics apart and figuring out how they worked. Soon he had built something – a homemade battery made of acid, metal and tape that could power the lights in one home.

DJ Focus

Next, Kelvin built a radio transmitter, a hand-powered generator and an audio mixer to create his own portable radio station. At 13, Kelvin began broadcasting under the name 'DJ Focus'. "If you can focus you can do an invention perfectly," Kelvin said. Before long, national radio and television stations in Sierra Leone wanted to interview Kelvin. The interviews attracted the attention of the prestigious Massachusetts Institute of Technology (MIT) in the USA, which invited Kelvin on a Visiting Practitioners' Program. Here, Kelvin met and designed electronic devices with other engineers. His experience at MIT was recorded on YouTube and received over ten million views.

Freetown, Sierra Leone

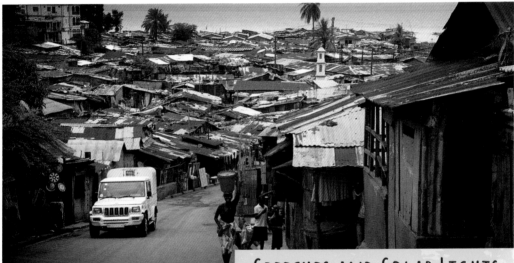

ACHIEVEMENTS

• Youngest-ever participant of MIT's Visiting Practitioners' Program

• Winner of Global Minimum's Innovate Salone Competition, 2012

• Honorary member of Emergency USA (provider of free medical care to victims of war or poverty)

Speeches and Solar Lights

After his stay at MIT, Kelvin was invited to speak at Harvard University and at the Technology, Entertainment, Design (TED) conference, which streams talks by inspiring people online. Kelvin's story was reported across the US media. Today, Kelvin lives and works in Canada, where he is developing a new solar light and phone charger for less developed countries. Kelvin continues to speak at conferences and seminars and uses his high profile to raise political issues, including improving the level of education in Africa.

Jazz Jennings

NAME: Jazz Jennings
BORN: 2000
PLACE OF BIRTH: Florida, USA
ROLE: Activist and spokesperson
for transgender rights

Toys and Dresses

From an early age, Jazz Jennings' parents felt there was something different about their youngest child. Jazz had always liked girls' toys more than boys and loved wearing dresses. For the Jennings, this was no cause for concern. After all, lots of boys enjoy dressing up. But when Jazz turned two, he started referring to himself as a 'she' and insisted that his penis was a mistake. "When's the good fairy going to come with her magic wand and change, you know, my genitalia?" Jazz asked his mother, Jeanette.

> "I'm honestly the luckiest kid in the world. Without her [Jazz's Mum, Jeanette] I wouldn't be able to be the proud, confident transgender woman that I am today."

Doctor's Diagnosis

Jazz's parents decided to consult a doctor who said Jazz had a condition called Gender Dysphoria. This means that a person does not identify with the gender they were given at birth. Jazz was born a boy, but identified as a girl. Today, this is more commonly known as transgender. The doctor said Jazz should be allowed to live as a girl, or he could suffer from depression. "When she insisted very early on that she was a girl, I thought it was a phase at first," said Jeanette Jennings. "But she was persistent, insistent and consistent, which are three signs of a transgender child."

Principals and Papers

Jazz could be treated like a girl at home, but what would happen when she went to school? Jazz's parents tried to explain to her school that Jazz was transgender and needed to live as a girl. But the school would not accept it at first. So Jeanette went to the local newspaper with Jazz's story. The newspaper article convinced the school to take Jazz's parents' requests seriously, although Jazz felt that change was slow in coming. Her story, however, had attracted interest elsewhere. Barbara Walters, one of America's most famous television journalists, wanted to interview Jazz. Aged just seven years old, Jazz would soon become the world's most famous transgender child.

Transgender Spokesperson

The Barbara Walters interview in 2007 made Jazz Jennings not only famous, but also a spokesperson for transgender rights. Other families with transgender children got in touch to share their stories. The Jennings decided to set up the TransKids Purple Rainbow Foundation, a charity that helps and supports transgender children. But despite the positive publicity for transgender rights, there was also a backlash.

Jazz with her family at the GLAAD Awards

"Every day I experience cyber-bullying, but I keep sharing my story ... in the face of constant ignorance and hatred I prefer to disregard negative options and continue moving forward with love."

Comments and Criticism

While Jazz enjoyed ongoing media attention, which included more interviews and a documentary by Oprah Winfrey, her mother was confronted with criticism. Some people sent threatening messages to the Jennings' home, while others wrote abusive comments online. Some accused Jazz's parents of committing child abuse by allowing Jazz to live as a girl.

Jazz at the 2016 Pride March in New York

TRANSGENDER FACTS AND FIGURES

- Over 1.4 million people in the USA identify as transgender
- Nearly 150,000 American teenagers identify as transgender
- In 2017, US president Donald Trump reversed a bill giving protection to transgender students
- By 2017, 20 countries had passed laws recognising the rights of transgender people.

Books and Bullying

Jazz's fame grew as she became a teenager. She wrote a children's book and two memoirs about being transgender. Today, Jazz also stars in a reality TV show, 'I am Jazz', about her family life and her journey to transition into a woman. But despite the fame and fortune, Jazz's life is not easy. She has to undergo surgery and take drugs to transition, and often suffers from harassment on social media. However, for Jazz, supporting and sharing the lives of the transgender community is more important than anything else.

Kiara Nirghin

Hello, my name is

Kiara

I love CHEMISTRY

DROUGHT WORLDWIDE

Kiara's work deals with drought. Scientists say drought brought about by climate change is one of the main environmental challenges facing the world this century. Every continent except North America experienced large areas of severe or extreme drought in 2017.

NAME: Kiara Nirghin
BORN: 2000
PLACE OF BIRTH: Johannesburg, South Africa
ROLE: Scientist and Inventor

Devastating Drought

In 2015, South Africa began one of its worst droughts in 30 years. The drought killed crops and livestock and brought water restrictions to homes. As the drought spread, over 40 million people in 17 countries were affected. But teenager Kiara Nirghin saw the drought as an opportunity. What the world needed was a way of storing water long term, so there was enough to survive periods of drought. Kiara's solution was a Super Absorbent Polymer (SAP) that sucks up water and can later be sprinkled on dry crops. But there was a twist: Kiara's SAP would be made from orange peel and avocado skins.

Orange Peel and Avocado Skins

With some experimenting, Kiara had discovered that orange peel and avocado skins could be turned into a SAP simply by applying heat and light from the Sun. Unlike many other SAPs, Kiara's mixture did not contain chemicals and was completely biodegradable. Better still, the ingredients came from the waste left over from juice companies, which made her SAP cheap to make.

No More Thirsty Crops

In 2016, Kiara submitted her SAP to the annual Google Science Fair – and won. The prize was a US$50,000 scholarship and the expertise of a Google business mentor to help Kiara. Today, Kiara's main aim is to help the drought-afflicted regions of her native South Africa: "If the idea was commercialised and applied to real farms and real crops I definitely think the impact that drought has on crops would be reduced. I wanted to minimise the effect that drought has on the community and the main thing it affects is the crops. That was the springboard for the idea," Kiara said.

"The only resources involved in the creation of the orange peel mixture were electricity and time, no special equipment or materials were required."

Anoyara Khatun

Stolen for Slavery

Anoyara Khatun was 12 years old when she was taken by human traffickers and forced to work as a domestic slave. She was driven hundreds of kilometres from her small village in the Sundarbans, West Bengal, to Delhi, the capital of India. Here, she was forced to work long hours as a maid for a rich family. The traffickers promised they would give Anoyara's pay to her family in the Sundarbans. But no money ever came. All her family knew was that Anoyara had gone missing one day.

NAME: Anoyara Khatun
BORN: 1996
PLACE OF BIRTH: Sundarbans, West Bengal, India
ROLE: Activist for Children's Rights

Dropping out to Work

Anoyara had not wanted to leave school, but she had little choice. When she was five, Anoyara's father died and the family was plunged into poverty. Anoyara's mother worked as a school cook, but this did not pay enough to support their family. When she turned 12, Anoyara decided to help. She left school and started looking for work. This was when the traffickers found Anoyara. Six months later Anoyara was trapped working in Delhi.

Many children in India are forced to work on building sites.

Trafficking Village

Unlike many children trafficked into forced labour, Anoyara escaped from the home she was working in. She was then discovered by the charity Save the Children, which sent Anoyara back to her family in the Sundarbans. Anoyara was now safe, but she realised that millions of children were not. She decided to dedicate herself to ending child slave labour and started with the children in her own village. It was going to be an uphill battle.

Child Labour

- Over 135,000 children are trafficked in India every year
- Between 6 and 12 million children in India are working in forced labour
- Over 150 million children worldwide work in forced conditions
- Many children work on farms and building sites and in factories.

Adults and Underage Armies

When Anoyara raised the issue of forced child labour in her village, few adults took her seriously. Many did not understand what kind of conditions their children were made to work in. Some parents living in poverty said they had little choice but to sell their children to traffickers. Others felt there was nothing wrong in arranging for their underage daughters to marry older men. Anoyara decided that if the adults in her village would not listen, then perhaps the children would. Soon she had formed a small army of child followers.

"I dream of a world where issues like child marriage, trafficking and any form of abuse won't be there."

Stopping the Traffickers

One night, Anoyara heard of a trafficker visiting a neighbour to convince them to sell their teenage daughter into marriage. She immediately assembled her child army to confront the trafficker and stop the marriage. After hearing of Anoyara's success, other children joined her. Together they stopped several traffickers from operating in Anoyara's village. Another time, the children blocked the way of the visiting education minister until he agreed to build more schools. Since then, over 80 new schools have been built in the Sundarbans.

(Right) Indian children and young people take part in a march against forced child labour in Kolkata, India in July 2018.

Education Re-enrollers

Today, Anoyara and her child army look out for traffickers who are out to trick families into selling their children. To date, Anoyara has stopped 85 attempts to traffic children, rescued 200 children from forced labour, saved more than 50 girls from forced marriages and helped re-enrol over 200 children back into education. Her work has made Anoyara an international spokesperson and activist for children's rights. She has spoken on the issue at the United Nations and in 2017 won the Nari Shakti Puraskhar Award for empowering women. Now Anoyara has 80 childrens' groups on the lookout for traffickers in West Bengal. Nothing makes Anoyara happier, she says, than rescuing a child.

"We try and persuade parents by giving them real examples of children who were sent to work and what happened to them. We tell them 'what do you care about? Money or your child?'... When we cannot convince parents we mobilise the local authorities who then come and investigate the cases and take action."

Shibby de Guzman

#Youth RESIST

DUTERTE'S DRUG WAR

Shibby has led protests against the Philippine President Rodrigo Duterte. After taking office in 2016, Duterte promised to kill drug criminals and urged Filipino citizens to kill drug addicts. Between 4,000 and 20,000 people have been killed so far without trial.

NAME: Shibby de Guzman
BORN: 2003
PLACE OF BIRTH: Manila, Philippines
ROLE: Political activist

PROTESTING THE PRESIDENT

Shibby de Guzman began protesting against the Philippine government when she was just 13 years old. The president, Rodrigo Duterte, had announced he would give former president Ferdinand Marcos a hero's burial. Marcos was a corrupt dictator who rigged elections and stole billions from his people during his 20 years in power. When the news was announced, Shibby started organising protest rallies. Here, demonstrators held banners saying 'Marcos is a traitor, Marcos is not a hero,' and burned photos of the late president (below).

"Please do not underestimate the youth. We completely know and understand the injustice we are protesting against."

DRUG DECLARATION

Speaking out against President Duterte is a risky business. In 2016, Duterte declared a war on drugs that has left thousands of Filipinos dead. Their bodies are left displaying signs saying 'drug lord' or 'drug pusher'. No-one knows how many innocent people have been killed. The United Nations and European Union have condemned Duterte's war on drugs as a 'crime under international law'. Few dared to speak out against Duterte, but Shibby would not be put off.

TOP TEENAGER

In 2017, Shibby led hundreds of students on a street protest against Duterte's drug war. Armed with a megaphone and signs reading 'We might all be taken for drug pushers', Shibby gained headlines around the world. She then made a speech before the crowd, saying that the Philippines would not support another dictator like President Marcos. Although criticised online by Duterte supporters, Shibby was named one of *TIME* magazine's 'Most Influential Teens of 2017' for her protesting efforts.

45

Muzoon Almellehan

Syrian refugees line up at a border crossing point in October 2015.

BECOMING REFUGEES

After two years of civil war in Syria, Muzoon Almellehan's father had had enough. In the city of Daraa it was now too dangerous for him to work as a teacher. "We thought at any moment we might die from one of the bombings," Muzoon said. Together, the 14-year-old Muzoon, her three siblings and her parents prepared to leave. They would travel by car to the neighbouring country of Jordan and then cross the border by foot after dark. There was a refugee camp there that should take them in. But first they had to survive the highly dangerous journey.

NAME: MUZOON ALMELLEHAN
BORN: 1999
PLACE OF BIRTH: DARAA, SYRIA
ROLE: ACTIVIST AND CAMPAIGNER FOR REFUGEE RIGHTS AND EDUCATION

Bag of Books

Muzoon's father had told his children to pack one small bag, but noticed Muzoon was struggling to carry hers. "My father said, 'Muzoon, what did you bring? It's really heavy.' I told him I'd packed my schoolbooks – I had more than ten of them. Nothing else. 'You are crazy,' he said." But Muzoon reasoned that if there was no school in Jordan, she could at least study with the books she had brought. "I was worried that if I lost my education, I'd lose everything," she said.

Marriage or School?

Muzoon's family reached the refugee camp of Za'atari safely, but the reality of the camp was a shock for Muzoon. There was no electricity or internet access, and water had to be fetched from a communal tank. Muzoon was pleased to find there was a school in the camp, but many of the children were not attending. Then she found out many of the girls in the camp – even those as young as 13 – were being married off. Many of the girls' parents believed this was a way of protecting their daughters from further harm. But Muzoon disagreed with them: "As refugees we needed education more than ever to face the challenges and suffering in our lives," she said.

Za'atari refugee camp

47

Muzoon's Mission

Muzoon decided to make it her mission to keep the girls in the Za'atari camp in school. She visited their families and explained the importance of education. She also told them that Syria needed a new generation of engineers, teachers and doctors to help rebuild the country when the war there ended. Muzoon was able to convince many girls to stay in school.

Muzoon and Malala

Muzoon's work caught the attention of the United Nations Children's Fund (UNICEF). The organisation sent Muzoon on a trip to Chad in Africa to speak to teenage girls living in refugee camps there. She was also asked to speak at the United Nations General Assembly and the G20 Summit. Before long, Muzoon was being called the 'Malala of Syria' (see pages 22–25) and met Malala herself at the Azraq refugee camp. Malala also invited Muzoon to attend the ceremony where Malala received her Nobel Peace Prize in 2014.

Syrian refugee girls in class at the Za'atari camp

"When people started calling me the Malala of Syria, I was so proud! And then when I actually met her? She is remarkable. We shared our stories, our souls, and our goals as education advocates, and we became really good friends."

English Education

In 2015, the Almellehan family was offered a chance to relocate to Newcastle, England. Muzoon was delighted to be able to leave the refugee camps and continue her education. But the cold weather was a shock and at first she found speaking English difficult. However, Muzoon said the school was very welcoming and asked the nine Syrian refugees it took in to tell their stories at a school assembly. Today, Muzoon wants to study political science and international relations at Newcastle University and hopes to one day return to Syria to rebuild there. "With all our voices, we can make a difference. Not just a small one – we can make a huge difference. We can change the world," Muzoon said.

(Left) Muzoon with Malala Yousafzai

REFUGEE CHILDREN AND EDUCATION

- Only 61 per cent of refugees worldwide attend school
- Only 1 per cent of refugee children go on to university
- Over 5.3 million people have had to flee Syria because of the war
- In 2017, 536,000 Syrian refugee children were not attending school in their new homelands of Jordan, Lebanon and Turkey.

Shubham Banerjee

NAME: Shubham Banerjee
BORN: 2001
PLACE OF BIRTH: Hasselt, Belgium
(emigrated at 4 to California, USA)
ROLE: Inventor of the Braille printer, Braigo

BLIND PRINTING

When Shubham Banerjee was 12 years old he asked his parents how blind people read. "Google it!" they answered. Shubham googled his question and learned blind people read by using Braille, a series of raised dots on paper which represent letters, numbers and words. But Shubham was shocked to discover a Braille printer cost over US$2,000 – too expensive for many blind readers. Shubham decided to build a low-cost Braille-printing printer – from LEGO®.

VISUALLY IMPAIRED PEOPLE WORLDWIDE

• 36 million people are completely blind
• 217 million people have severe or moderate visual impairment (MSVI)
• 253 million people are visually impaired
• 1.1 billion people have near-vision impairment.

BRAIGO FOR BRAILLE

It took Shubham seven weeks and many late nights at the kitchen table with his dad to create his printer. Using a LEGO® mindstorm EV3 robotics kit and some electrical parts, Shubham created a prototype machine that could print the six main dots used in Braille. He called his printer 'Braigo 1.0' after 'Braille' and 'LEGO®'. With a US$35,000 investment from his dad, Shubham was able to start his own company, Braigo Labs, and build an even better printer, Braigo 2.0. Braigo 2.0 can translate electronic text and print it in Braille.

INTEL INVESTMENT

Shubham's Braigo printers impressed the blind community and several computer companies, including Intel. Intel invested into Braigo Labs and gave Shubham their new Edison microchip to use in his printer. Today, Braigo Labs gives away the design and software for Braigo 1.0 for free. Shubham plans to release the Braigo 2.0 printer onto the market soon and sell it for around US$350. Shubham's printer has made him famous and his friends call him 'Braigo Boy'. However, Shubham said they don't treat him like a world-changing inventor: "They're pretty chill. They don't treat me differently."

Melati and Isabel Wijsen ⚡

"The question became: 'Who's going to do something about it?' We thought, 'Why don't we do something about it? Why don't we stand up for our island?'"

NAME: Melati and Isabel Wijsen
BORN: 2000 (Melati) and 2002 (Isabel)
PLACE OF BIRTH: Bali, Indonesia
ROLE: Plastic bag-banning activists

Bali beaches

One day at school, sisters Melati and Isabel Wijsen decided to declare war on plastic. Their lesson had been about inspirational leaders who had changed the world. But Melati and Isabel didn't want to wait till adulthood to change the world. Instead they decided to make a start on fighting the plastic clogging up the beaches of their island home of Bali.

PLASTIC POLLUTER

- Indonesia produces the equivalent of a 14-storey building of plastic rubbish every day
- Indonesia's plastic waste makes up 10 per cent of all plastic in the sea
- Only 5 per cent of plastic bags get recycled in Bali.

Swimming in Plastic

Bali is a tropical island with two seasons: dry and wet. But the winds of the wet season have also introduced a new event to Bali, known as 'trash season'. This is when plastic rubbish from the sea washes up on Bali's beaches. "When you're at the beach sunbathing or going for a swim, you're swimming with plastic, you're sunbathing with plastic. There's no escaping it," Melati said. The amount of rubbish is perhaps not surprising: Indonesia is a major plastic polluter, second only in the world to China.

Bye Bye Plastic Bags

Melati and Isabel founded an organisation called Bye Bye Plastic Bags (BBPB). Its mission was to ban the use, sale and production of plastic bags on Bali. To do this, the sisters aimed to collect signatures on a petition and present it to Bali's governor. They hoped this would convince the governor to change the local laws on plastic.

PLASTIC PETITION

After 18 months, Melati and Isabel had collected 100,000 signatures on their petition. But the governor would not meet with them. To force him to listen, the sisters went on a hunger strike that would only end when the governor agreed to meet them. In reality, the hunger strike only lasted between sunrise and sunset – but it proved effective. Just 24 hours later the governor invited the sisters to a meeting. He then signed a document promising to support the banning of plastic bags and introduce recyclable bags instead.

CAMPAIGN CLEAN-UP

Meeting the governor was only the first step for Melati and Isabel and the BBPB. Next, the Wijsen sisters launched a campaign that rewards plastic-free shops in Bali by promoting them on the BBPB website. Then, the sisters set up a 'pilot village', where they distributed 1,000 recyclable bags to villagers and local shops to use instead of plastic bags. The sisters also organised Bali's largest ever beach clean-up, which attracted over 12,000 volunteers.

ACHIEVEMENTS

- Winners of the Our Earth Bambi Award, 2017
- Named Forbes Indonesia's Most Inspiring Women of 2017
- Over 1 million online views of the Wijsen sisters' TED Talk video
- Over 150 events spoken at
- More than 1,000 booklets donated to schools.

CLIMATE AND CHANGE-MAKERS

Today BBPB is a global movement with teams campaigning for the ban of plastic bags in 17 different countries. Melati and Isabel have also become internationally famous and travel around the world to speak at conferences, schools and even the United Nations. The sisters have spoken to over 16,000 students in 12 different countries and have produced an educational booklet about climate change and ocean plastic. "We believe that through education you can raise an entire generation of change-makers. The generation today is ready to be part of the solution and they are also motivated, passionate and willing," Isabel said. Melati and Isabel hope that their fight to make Bali a 'plastic-bag free province' will encourage other countries to do the same.

Easton LaChappelle

"I was the kid who took apart everything I got when I was little – I had so much curiosity about how things worked. I loved creating and having the freedom that there's really no right or wrong way to make something."

NAME: Easton LaChappelle
BORN: 1995
PLACE OF BIRTH: Rhinebeck, New York, USA
ROLE: Inventor

Fair robotics

When he was 14 years old, Easton LaChappelle built his first robotic arm using LEGO®, fishing wire, electrical tubing and a 3D printer. He then showed his arm at a science fair. At the fair, Easton noticed a young girl paying the arm special attention. After speaking to her, Easton found that the girl had a prosthetic arm which had cost US$80,000. It had almost been too much for the girl's family to afford. This inspired Easton to turn his robotic arm into a device that was cheaper and better than other prosthetic arms on the market.

Mind control

Easton's main challenge was to enable his robotic arm to be controlled by the human brain. To do this, Easton bought a computer game called Mindflex. The game apparently allowed players to control a ball with their mind. Easton used the game to work out how certain movements were linked to particular brainwaves. He then used this software in his robotic arm so it could be controlled by the wearer's brain. The final step was to upload the programme for the robotic arm to the internet, so that anyone with a 3D printer could download it and make their own arm.

EASTON'S ROBOTIC ARM

- Weighs 0.5 kg
- Has individual finger movement
- Has a battery life of three to four days
- Has realistic, paintable fingernails.

Printers and presidents

Easton's robotic arm made an instant impact. Easton was invited to give seminars and talks about his robotic arm and even used it to shake hands with then US president Barack Obama (far left). Next, he was invited to work with NASA on their robotics programme. When he turned 17, Easton founded his own company Unlimited Tomorrow, which creates robotic prosthetic limbs. Today, Easton is working on an exoskeleton that will help paraplegics walk again. The key, Easton says, is for all of his creations to be easily downloadable and affordable for the people who need them.

Sarah Sobka

NAME: Sarah Sobka
BORN: 1998
PLACE OF BIRTH: Sheffield, England
ROLE: Scientist

SCIENCE AND DISEASE

When Sarah Sobka was 17 years old she jumped at the chance to present her research at a leading science competition. Sarah's research was about treating cystic fibrosis, an incurable disease that clogs sufferers' lungs with thick, sticky mucus, making it hard to breathe. While at high school, Sarah had wondered if a drug for Irritable Bowl Syndrome could also be used to treat cystic fibrosis. When she learned Sheffield University was investigating the drug, Lubiprostone, Sarah asked if she could help.

CYSTIC FIBROSIS

- 1 in 25 people carry the gene causing cystic fibrosis
- People with cystic fibrosis often need to take over 50 pills a day
- There is currently no cure for cystic fibrosis.

RESEARCH ATTACHMENT

After speaking to Sarah, Sheffield University's Dr Robson allowed her to work with her team on their investigation into Lubiprostone. After examining the disease in the university's laboratory, Sarah realised she had become "attached to cystic fibrosis". She decided to pursue a career in medical research and dedicate herself to treatment of the disease. "I loved the fact that I was able to play a small role in a larger piece of work that could improve the lives of people suffering from cystic fibrosis."

SCIENCE SHORTLIST

In 2015, Sarah's research made the shortlist of the National Science + Engineering Competition – an annual event that showcases the science projects of pupils between 11 and 18 years of age. In 2015, there were a total of 2,000 entrants. Sarah was therefore stunned when she won the whole competition and was named UK Young Scientist of the Year. "I thought it would be amazing to have been chosen as 'Runner up' but still had not contemplated the idea that I might have won," she said. Today, Sarah is studying medicine and hopes her achievements will help inspire other young women to take up roles in science.

Lisa Ranran Hu

"I'd like to let everyone have a better understanding of the LGBT community through my film. I feel like I have a sense of mission."

NAME: Lisa Ranran Hu
BORN: 1999
PLACE OF BIRTH: Beijing, China
ROLE: Film director

Transgender awareness

In 2016, teenager Lisa Ranran Hu decided to make a film about being transgender in China. The film, *Escape*, followed a school-age boy who thinks of himself as a girl and struggles with life as a result. Lisa believed a film needed to be made to raise awareness of transgender people living in Chinese society. "I wanted to speak for transgenders and acquaint more people with this disadvantaged group. Many people regard transgenders as very different. I wanted to make this film to tell people that they are as normal as anyone else," Lisa said.

LGBT RIGHTS IN CHINA

- Same-sex relationships were made legal in 1997
- In 2001, homosexuality was no longer classified as a mental illness
- Same-sex couples are still unable to marry or adopt children
- There are no laws to protect LGBT people from harassment or discrimination.

Teenage crew

Lisa's film was controversial for two reasons. The first was because Lisa had only ever directed two short films and her teenage crew had never worked in film before. Lisa describes herself as a 'self-taught director' and her crew were simply volunteers from school. They made the costumes and sets themselves and shot much of the film at their high school. But *Escape* was also controversial because of attitudes to the Lesbian, Gay, Bisexual and Transgender (LGBT) community in China. In particular, the Chinese government had recently banned showing same-sex relationships on television and online videos.

Audience acceptance

Escape was difficult for many to accept. Lisa's school would not show the film at its film festival, although it supported Hu to make it. It had limited screenings and has sold only around 100 copies on DVD, but *Escape* won the attention of LGBT groups within China and a larger audience overseas. The film also secured Lisa a place at the University of California in the USA, and saw her named one of *TIME* magazine's most influential teenagers of 2017. Lisa said, "After I complete my studies and return to China, I want to work to change Chinese movies and even Chinese society ... our film has really changed some people's attitudes toward sexual minorities and even themselves. This is what I want,"

Further information

WEBSITES

To find out more about some of the Teen Pioneers in this book, you can visit their websites at the addresses below:

Sonita Alizadeh's website features information about her life and child marriages worldwide:
https://www.sonita.org

Mikaila Ulmer's Me & the Bees website explains how her lemonade is saving bees around the world:
https://www.meandthebees.com

Mary Grace Henry's Reverse the Course website helps educate underprivileged African girls by raising money through making and selling headbands: http://www.reversethecourse.org

Campbell Remess's Project365 provides information on how Campbell raises money for cancer by making teddy bears:
https://project365.org

Malala Yousafzai's Malala Fund website explains how people can break the barriers that prevent 130 million girls worldwide going to school:
https://www.malala.org

Yash Gupta's Sight Learning website explains how he is providing glasses to people who cannot afford them:
https://sightlearning.com

Jazz Jennings is co-founder of the Trans Kids Purple Rainbow Foundation which raises awareness about the lives of transgender children. Visit the Foundation's website at:
http://www.transkidspurplerainbow.org

Shubham Banerjee's invention of Braigo, a low-cost braille printer, is explored in depth on his website:
https://www.shu.today

Melati and Isabel Wijsen explain how they intend to rid the world of plastic bags on their Bye Bye Plastic Bags website: http://www.byebyeplasticbags.org

Easton LaChappelle's company Unlimited Tomorrow allows users to download files to build their own prosthetic robot arms. You can visit the website here:
http://theroboarm.com

BOOKS

Read about other people who have changed the world here:

Heroic Leaders and Activists (Brilliant Women), Georgia Amson-Bradshaw, Wayland, 2019

From Prejudice to Pride: A History of LGBTQ+ Movement, Amy Lame, Wayland, 2019

Suffragettes and the Fight for the Vote, Sarah Ridley, Franklin Watts, 2019

10 People that Changed the World, Ben Hubbard, Wayland, 2015

NOTE TO PARENTS AND TEACHERS:

Every effort has been made by the publisher to ensure that these websites contain no inappropriate or offensive material. However, because of the nature of the Internet, it is impossible to guarantee that the content of these sites will not be altered. We strongly advise that Internet access is supervised by a responsible adult.

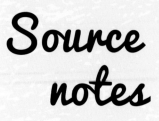

Source notes

Sonita Alizadeh p.6: 'The older generations': Deborah Bloom, Oct 13, 2015, CNN: edition.cnn.com/2015/10/11/world/afghanistan-rapper-sonita-alizadeh/index.html **p.8:** 'Brides for Sale', Sonita Alizadeh

Rene Silva p.13: 'It [the newspaper] says': Flora Charner, Al Jazeera, 8 Jun, 2014: www.aljazeera.com/indepth/features/2014/06/community-media-makes-waves-brazil-favelas-201467114934619488.html **p.15:** 'When I was younger': Rafael Johns, Youth Radio as reported in the Huffington Post, Dec 6, 2017: www.huffingtonpost.com/youth-radio-youth-media-international/one-teens-news-startup-in_b_8842358.html

Mary Grace Henry p.16: 'The greatest obstacle': 23 September, 2014, World of Children Website interview: worldofchildren.org/honoree/mary-grace-henry/

Salvador Gómez Colón p.18: 'One day should not': Time Staff, Nov 3, 2017, Time Magazine: time.com/5003930/most-influential-teens-2017/

Campbell Remess p.20: 'The magic in': The Edge Magazine, Dec 21, 2017: www.theedgeleaders.com/campbell-remess/ **p.21:** 'I decided to make': CNN, 2017: edition.cnn.com/videos/tv/2017/12/15/cnnheroes-remess.cnn/video/playlists/2017-top-10-cnn-heroes/] **p.21** 'I've got to put it': Elise Fantin, 6 Nov, 2016, ABC news: www.abc.net.au/news/2016-11-06/young-hobart-teddy-bear-maker-wins-hearts-across-the-globe/7998972

Malala Yousafzai p.23: 'I am not here': Malala Yousafzai to the UN, Jul 12, 2003: theirworld.org/explainers/malala-yousafzais-speech-at-the-youth-takeover-of-the-united-nations **p.23:** 'How dare the Taliban': Naomi Blumberg, Jul

8, 2018, Encyclopedia Britannica: www.britannica.com/biography/Malala-Yousafzai **p.24:** 'One child, one teacher': Malala Yousafzai to the UN, Jul 12, 2003: theirworld.org/explainers/malala-yousafzais-speech-at-the-youth-takeover-of-the-united-nations **p.25:** 'I think they may be regretting': Mishal Husain, Oct 7, 2013, BBC Magazine: www.bbc.co.uk/news/magazine-24379018

Yash Gupta p.27: 'I think there's a misconception': Erika Clarke and Kathleen Toner, Sep 5, 2013, CNN: edition.cnn.com/2013/09/05/health/cnnheroes-gupta-glasses/index.html

Joshua Wong p.31: 'They can lock up': Jan 17, 2018, BBC News: www.bbc.co.uk/news/world-asia-china-42714022 **p.31:** 'Hong Kong Can't Yet': Kevin Lui, Nov 6, 2017, Time Magazine: time.com/5011057/hong-kong-joshua-wong-interview/

Kelvin Doe p.32: 'Creativity is universal': Kelvin Doe speaking at TEDxTeen: www.youtube.com/watch?v=4aQ2h3VaC3c **p.32:** 'The lights would come on': Hayley Hudson, Nov 19, 2012, Huffington Post: www.huffingtonpost.co.uk/entry/kelvin-doe-self-taught-en_n_2159735?guccounter=1&guce_referrer_us=aHR0cHM6Ly93d3cuZ29vZ2xlLmNvbS88&guce_referrer_cs=UyKN-QPjBLCPOshvc5DYuQ **p.33:** 'If you focus': Hayley Hudson, Nov 19, 2012, Huffington Post: www.huffingtonpost.co.uk/entry/kelvin-doe-self-taught-en_n_2159735?guccounter=1&guce_referrer_us=aHR0cHM6Ly93d3cuZ29vZ2xlLmNvbS88&guce_referrer_cs=UyKN-QPjBLCPOshvc5DYuQ]

Jazz Jennings p.35: 'When's the good fairy': Jazz Jennings, May 31, 2016, Time Magazine: time.com/4350574/jazz-jennings-transgender/ **p.35:** 'I'm honestly the luckiest': Diana Tourjee, May 7, 2018, Vice: broadly.vice.com/en_us/article/a3y58e/jazz-jennings-mom-jeanette-interview **p.35:** 'When she insisted very early on': Diana Tourjee, May 7, 2018, Vice: broadly.vice.com/en_us/article/a3y58e/jazz-jennings-mom-jeanette-interview **p.36:** Tweet by Jazz Jennings

Kiara Nirghin p.39: 'The only resources': Aug 15, 2016, CNN: edition.cnn.com/2016/08/09/africa/orange-drought-kiara-nirghin/index.html **p.39:** 'If the idea was commercialised': Sep 28, 2016, BBC: www.bbc.co.uk/news/world-africa-37497682

Anoyara Khatun p.42: 'I dream of a world': Anoyara Khatun on the Save The Children Website: campaigns.savethechildren.net/blogs/tanuanand/meet-anoyara-our-child-delegate-unga71 **p.43:** 'We try and persuade parents': Nita Bhalla, Mar 9, 2017, Thomson Reuters Foundation: www.globalcitizen.org/en/content/child-trafficking-anoyara-khatun-women-power-award/

Shibby de Guzman p.45: 'Please do not underestimate': Janvic Mateo, Nov 3, 2017, The Philippine Star: www.philstar.com/headlines/2017/11/03/1755505/anti-marcos-student-joins-times-most-influential-teens-list

Muzoon Almellehan p.46: 'We thought at any moment': Maggie Mertens, Oct 30, 2017 Glamour: www.glamour.com/story/women-of-the-year-2017-muzoon-almellehan **p.47:** 'My father said': Muzoon Almellehan from TEDx talk: www.vexplode.com/en/tedx/why-i-carried-my-school-books-out-of-syria-muzoon-almellehan-tedxlondonsalon/ **p.47:** 'As refugees we needed': Muzoon Almellehan: from TEDx talk: www.vexplode.com/en/tedx/why-i-carried-my-school-books-out-of-syria-muzoon-almellehan-tedxlondonsalon **p.48:** 'When people started calling me': Maggie Mertens, Oct 30, 2017 Glamour: www.glamour.com/story/women-of-the-year-2017-muzoon-almellehan **p.49:** 'With all our voices': Muzoon Almehellan, Nov 19, 2017, Washington Post: www.washingtonpost.com/opinions/i-fled-syria-years-ago-refugee-children-like-me-cant-give-up-on-education/2017/11/19/78046398-cb23-11e7-8321-481fd63f174d_story.html?utm_term=.b82934bf0148

Shubham Banerjee p.51: 'They're pretty chill': Brittany Shoot, Sep 18, 2015, Smithsonian.com: www.smithsonianmag.com/innovation/meet-13-year-old-who-invented-low-cost-braille-printer-180956659/

Melati Wijsen p.52: 'The question became': Eden Gillespie, Jun 1, 2017, Forbes Indonesia: medium.com/@edengillespie/melati-and-isabel-wijsen-forbes-indonesia-100-inspiring-women-39ac5bbcdaec **p.53:** 'When you're at the beach': Eden Gillespie, Jun 1, 2017, Forbes Indonesia: medium.com/@edengillespie/melati-and-isabel-wijsen-forbes-indonesia-100-inspiring-women-39ac5bbcdaec **p.55:** 'We believe that: Anastasia W. Wibowo, Nov 22, 2017, Indonesia Tatler: www.indonesiatatler.com/society/tatler-talented-teens-melati-and-isabel-wijsen-say-no-to-plastic-bags

Easton LaChappelle p.57: 'I was the little kid': Alejandro Alba, Oct 20, 2017, Men's Health: www.menshealth.com/health/a19539309/easton-lachappelle-3d-printed-prosthetic-limbs/]

Sarah Sobka p.59: 'I loved the fact': interview with the Nuffield Foundation: www.nuffieldfoundation.org/sarah-sobka **p.59:** 'I thought it would be amazing': Joty Chopra, Mar 18, 2015, The Huffington Post: www.huffingtonpost.co.uk/2015/03/18/uk-young-scientist-of-the-year-sarah-sobka_n_6893750.html

Lisa Ranran Hu p.60: 'I'd like to let everyone': Tang Yucheng, Aug 18, 2017, NY Times: www.nytimes.com/2017/08/18/world/asia/china-transgender-film-school.html **p.61:** 'I wanted to speak for transgenders': Tang Yucheng, Aug 18, 2017, NY Times: www.nytimes.com/2017/08/18/world/asia/china-transgender-film-school.html **p.61:** 'After I complete': Tang Yucheng, Aug 18, 2017, NY Times: www.nytimes.com/2017/08/18/world/asia/china-transgender-film-school.html]

Index